Solar System Explorers

Jupiter

Written by E.C. Andrews

KidHaven PUBLISHING

Published in 2026 by
KidHaven Publishing, an Imprint of
Greenhaven Publishing, LLC
2544 Clinton St., Buffalo, NY 14224

Written by: E.C. Andrews
Edited by: Noah Leatherland
Designed by: Amelia Harris

All facts, statistics, web addresses, and URLs in this book were verified as valid and accurate at time of writing. No responsibility for any changes to external websites or references can be accepted by either the author or publisher.

Cataloging-in-Publication Data
Names: Andrews, E.C.
Title: Jupiter / E.C. Andrews.
Description: Buffalo, NY : Kidhaven Publishing, 2026. | Series: Solar System Explorers | Includes glossary and index
Identifiers: ISBN 9781534549760 (pbk) | ISBN 9781534549777 (library bound) | ISBN 9781534549784 (ebook)
Subjects: LCSH: Jupiter (Planet)—Juvenile Literature
Classification: LCC QB661 A53 2026 | DDC 523.45 --dc25

Manufactured in the United States of America

CPSIA compliance information: Batch #CSKH26
For further information contact Greenhaven Publishing LLC
at 1-844-317-7404.

Please visit our website,
www.greenhavenpublishing.com.
For a free color catalog of all our high-quality books, call toll free 1-844-317-7404
or fax 1-844-317-7405.

Find us on

Image Credits

Images are courtesy of Shutterstock.com. With thanks to Getty Images, Thinkstock Photo and iStockphoto. Cover – AspctStyle, andreysharonov, aappp, Pike-28. Recurring Images – thomas eder, YummyBuum, Sabelskaya. 4–5 – Withan Tor, Artsiom P. 6–7 – buradaki, bilgeari. 8–9 – Vadim Sadovski, NASA images. 10–11 – AspctStyle. 12–13 – Artsiom P, Vadim Sadovski. 14–15 – Evgeniyqw, Dotted Yeti, Vlad Ra27. 16–17 – Artsiom P, Will hilton-kent. 18–19 – muratart, NASA/JPL/DLR, Public domain, via Wikimedia Commons. 20–21 – NASA/JPL, Public domain, via Wikimedia Commons, NASA, Public domain, via Wikimedia Commons. 22–23 – oobqoo.

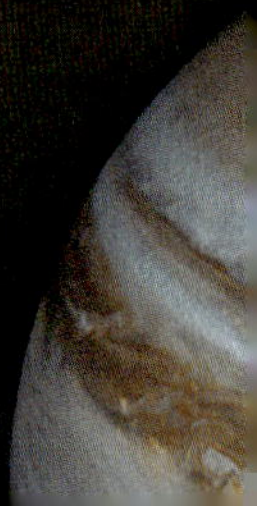

Contents

Words that look like **this** can be found in the glossary on page 24.

Let's Explore!

The solar system is made up of planets and objects that **orbit** a star called the sun. Have you ever wondered what those planets might be like? Join us on our mission to find out!

There are eight planets and five dwarf planets in the solar system. The solar system is a big place with lots of things to explore. But we explorers are up for the challenge.

Where Is Jupiter?

Each planet in the solar system orbits the sun at different distances. If we lined all the planets up in order of distance from the sun, it would look a bit like this:

Jupiter is in between Mars and Saturn. It is about 484 million miles (778 million km) from the sun. Jupiter is the fifth planet from the sun. Can you work out how many planets are even farther from the sun?

Round and Round

It takes Earth about 365 days to orbit the sun once. An orbit is how people measure years. A year on Jupiter is 4,333 Earth days long. That is about 12 Earth years!

As planets orbit, they spin on an **axis**. This is how days are measured. Jupiter has the shortest days in the solar system. It only takes about 10 hours for Jupiter to complete one spin.

Planet Profile

Here are some notes on Jupiter from our database.

Temperature

Jupiter is about minus 234 degrees Fahrenheit (-145°C).

Size

- Around: 235,298 miles (378,675 km)
- Across: 88,846 miles (142,984 km)

Water freezes at 32°F (0°C).

Water boils at 212°F (100°C).

What Is Jupiter Made Of?

Jupiter is a type of planet called a **gas** giant. Gas giants are made of gas and **liquid**. Jupiter is mostly made of gases called hydrogen and helium.

Jupiter's layers swirl and mix together.

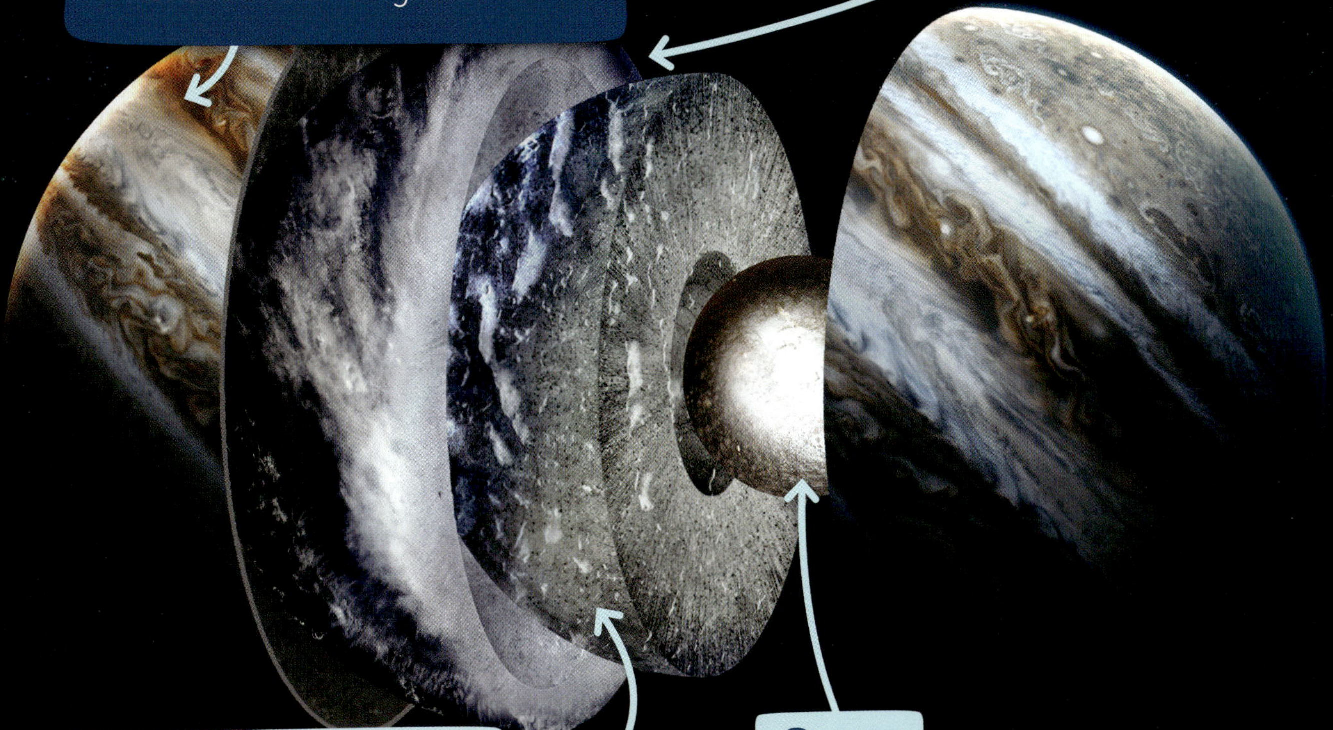

Outer Atmosphere

Jupiter's outer **atmosphere** is made of different gases.

Inner Atmosphere

Below the gases, the inner atmosphere is probably a huge ocean of liquid hydrogen.

Deep Atmosphere

The deep atmosphere is very hot – 43,000 ° F (24,000 ° C).

Core

Jupiter's core is either solid, or like a thick, hot soup.

Watching the Weather

Jupiter is a very cold place. It is also one of the stormiest planets in the solar system. The swirly patterns that we can see on Jupiter are actually huge storm clouds.

The Great Red Spot is a storm on Jupiter that has been going for over 150 years. The strong winds in the Great Red Spot are thought to reach over 375 miles (600 km) per hour.

Is There Life on Jupiter?

A habitable planet is a planet that living things can **survive** on. For now, Jupiter is not a habitable planet. It is much too cold. There is no water and the air is not breathable.

However, Jupiter has moons that could be habitable. One of Jupiter's moons is called Europa. Some scientists think Europa could support life as it has a huge ocean of water.

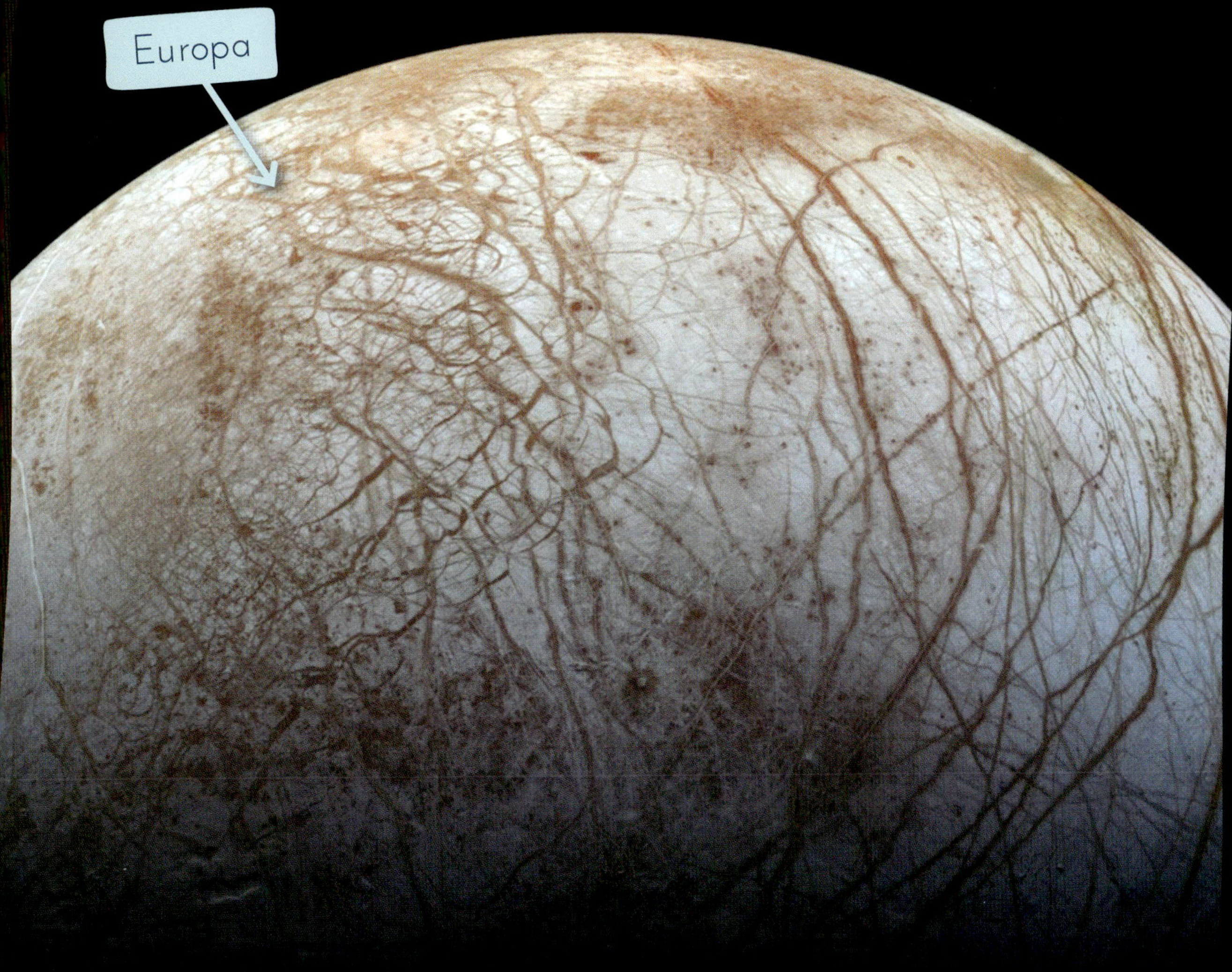

Spot the Satellites

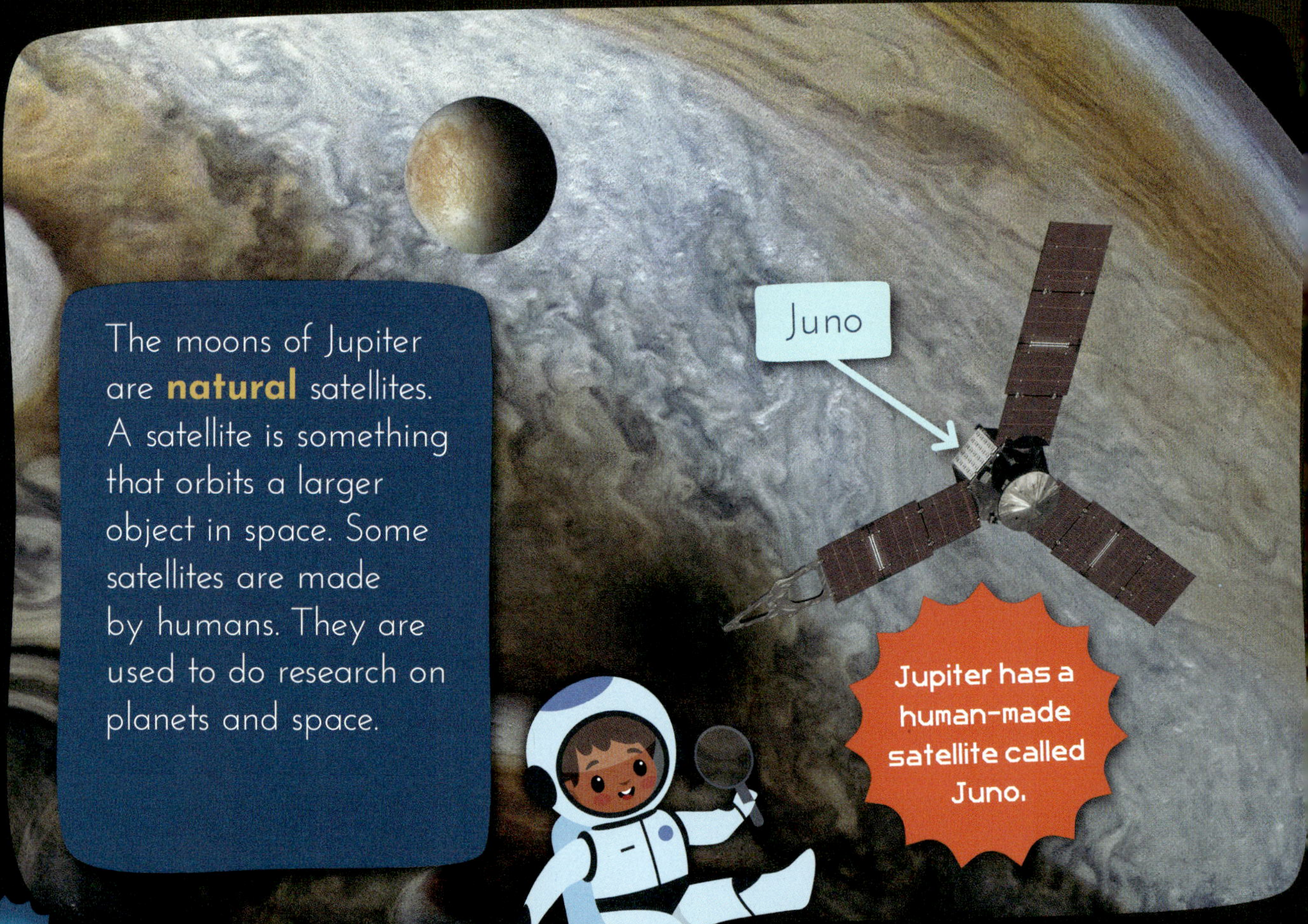

The moons of Jupiter are **natural** satellites. A satellite is something that orbits a larger object in space. Some satellites are made by humans. They are used to do research on planets and space.

Jupiter has a human-made satellite called Juno.

Jupiter has 95 moons that we know of. The largest moons (below) orbit closer to the planet. Some of the small, outer moons orbit in the opposite direction to Jupiter's spin. This is called a retrograde orbit.

The Jovian System

Jupiter is the biggest planet in the solar system. It is part of a place in the solar system called the Jovian system. Planets in the Jovian system are similar to Jupiter.

The Jovian system includes the solar system's four gas giants – Jupiter, Saturn, Uranus, and Neptune. The Jovian planets all have natural satellites, such as rings and moons.

Rings are pieces of rock and dust that orbit a planet.

More to Explore

What an incredible planet Jupiter is! We have had a wonderful time exploring the solar system's largest planet. We have learned so many new things. What did you learn about Jupiter today?

Now that we have finished our mission on Jupiter, it is time to explore a new place in the solar system. There are many more planets to explore. Our database is not going to fill itself!

Glossary

atmosphere	the mixture of gases that makes up the air and surrounds a planet
axis	an imaginary line that something turns on
degrees	a measuring unit used to explain how hot or cold something is
gas	a thing that is like air, which fills any space available
liquid	a material that flows, such as water
natural	found in nature and not made by people
orbit	move around a star or planet in a curved path
survive	to stay alive

Index